THE GREYEST TALE ON THE YUKON TRAIL

The Right to Be Treated Fairly No Matter What Colour You Are

Written by Dustin Milligan • Illustrated by Cory Tibbits

DC Canada Education Publishing

Written by: Dustin Milligan

Illustrated by: Cory Tibbits

Editors: Leonard Judge, Debbie Gervais

Copy Editor: Anja Pujic

Cover Design: Meredith Luce

Published in 2013 by: DC Canada Education Publishing

130 Slater Street, Suite 960
Ottawa, On, Canada K1P 6E2
www.dc-canada.ca

· ·

**We acknowledge the financial support of the Government of Canada
through the Canada Book Fund for our publishing activities.**

The Greyest Tale on the Yukon Trail

ISBN: 978-1-926776-55-2

· ·

Library and Archives Canada Cataloguing in Publication
Milligan, Dustin, 1984-
The greyest tale on the Yukon Trail : the right to be treated
fairly no matter what colour you are / written by Dustin Milligan
; illustrated by Cory Tibbits.
(The Charter for children)
ISBN 978-1-926776-56-9 (bound).--ISBN 978-1-926776-55-2 (pbk.)
1. Race discrimination--Canada--Juvenile literature.
2. Canada. Canadian Charter of Rights and Freedoms--
Juvenile literature. I. Tibbits, Cory II. Title. III. Series: Charter
for children
FC105.R32M54 2013   j323.171   C2013-901706-2

Preface

The idea for *The Charter for Children* first emerged when I was a student at the Faculty of Law at McGill University. After my first year of studies, I was concerned that the common citizen wasn't equipped to understand our country's complicated legal system—one that I myself had only begun to comprehend. Children are at a further disadvantage in this regard, as they have limited capacity, strength and knowledge of their rights. Combining these concerns with my love for literature and the law, I took on this large project—writing a series of books that offer children a basic understanding of the *Canadian Charter of Rights and Freedoms*.

I would like to thank the Faculty of Law of McGill University, and most notably, Professor Shauna Van Praagh, who provided guidance during the course of much of this project and without whom the project would not have been possible. I would also like to thank those who have contributed their thoughts, insights, encouragement, time and puns—most notably, my three friends, Dorian Needham, Malcolm Dort and Josie Marks; Danielle Downing and the students at King George Public School; Jessica Duarte; Gregory Ko; Faizel Gulamhussein; Jean-Simon Farrah; Anton Suphal; Sachin Aggarwal; Jonathan Odumeru; Hana Boye; Bhreagh Dabbs; Georgina Murphy; the wonderful team at DC Canada Education Publishing; and my incredible family, Keith, Deborah, Olivia, Christian, Jolene and Shawn.

This series is dedicated to the children of Canada—may your voices be heard and considered, and may your childhoods be filled with respect and dignity.

Dustin Milligan

In a time not so long ago, in Dawson City, Yukon, there lived a dog named Sam HusGee.

Every morning, Sam joined a pack of dogs for husky practice. They were all dogsled runners. They called themselves The Gold Mush.

Ever since he was a young pup, Sam dreamed of leading The Gold Mush.

Sam barked:

For all my years it's been my dream,
(In doggy years, that's seventeen).
Through snow and storms and summer's green,
I've trained to lead our dogsled team!

Sam had indeed trained hard.

His personal trainer was Dogavan Bailey. He was one of the best trainers in the mushing business.

Dogavan had seen potential in Sam from an early age. With Dogavan's coaching and all Sam's training, they were determined that Sam would lead a team to Yukon Gold.

Each morning, Sam sped by his teammates at practice. The others were left in the dust (of snow that is).

The Yukon Quest approached. It was the biggest dogsled race in all of Canada.

The Ministry of Dogsled Affairs chose which husky would lead each team in the Quest.

The Lead Dog Rule said:

> *The fastest husky, with the greatest ability,*
> *Will be chosen lead dog by the Ministry.*

Sam HusGee was the fastest husky on the team. He was the clear and obvious choice to lead The Gold Mush.

One cold December day, the members of The Gold Mush lined up in a row. It was selection day. Officer Pawmela Barksley of the Ministry of Dogsled Affairs was there to pick the lead dog.

As she circled the pack, the huskies were sure that Sam would be chosen to lead.

With frost on her breath, Officer Pawmela barked:

> *As all huskies know, grey dogs are quite slow,*
> *They've never won gold in the Yukon snow.*
> *To ensure that a pro, leads the Gold Mush row,*
> *I choose that brown husky named Sour-Toe!*

The entire pack was shocked at the choice.

Later that morning, Sam arrived home with floppy ears. His heart ached. He knew that he was the fastest husky on the team.

After throwing his gym bag on the floor, he turned on his computer. He searched online through old newspaper articles from *The Globe and Trail.*

As he read, he was reminded of the sad history of grey huskies in the Yukon. Years ago, grey huskies weren't allowed to become dogsled runners. They weren't allowed to run on the trails.

Sam clicked through article upon article of *The Globe and Trail*.

For years, the grey huskies demanded that they be allowed to run on the trails like the dogs of other colours.

It was only after many years of protest that an officer of the Ministry had barked:

> *From this day onwards,*
> *These trails will be fair!*
> *There'll be no ill treatment,*
> *Based on colour of hair!*

Grey huskies could finally mush on the trails.

But even though grey huskies were finally able to mush on the trails, there was a stereotype that still caused much harm.

Many dogs still believed that all grey huskies were slow.

Grey huskies hadn't been allowed to use the trails for many years so they didn't have the same training as the other dogs.

Each year, it was white, brown or black huskies that led their teams to gold medals in the Yukon Quest. There were pro-athletes of all other colours, but none were grey.

Sam thought about what Officer Pawmela had said that morning.

She had barked:

> *As all huskies know, grey dogs are quite slow,*
> *They've never won gold in the Yukon snow.*
> *To ensure that a pro, leads the Gold Mush row,*
> *I choose that brown husky named Sour-Toe!*

Officer Pawmela had assumed Sam was slow simply because he was a grey husky.

The bone rang. It was Sam's personal trainer, Dogavan Bailey.

Dogavan barked:

I have to declare that choice was unfair!
You were overlooked because of your hair!
Although you have speed, they don't like our breed,
Pawmela refused to choose a grey dog to lead.

Sam had heard this stereotype throughout his life.

As a young pup, he tried playing with the dogs of other colours. But as he chased cars or fetched sticks, the others would call him names.

They would say:

> *Grey-haired mutts are as slow as molasses!*
> *Sam HusGee will never mush the fastest!*

Their laughter made Sam want to train even harder.

Sam and Dogavan were tired of dealing with the stereotype that grey huskies were slow.

Sam barked:

> *We cannot sit and drool,*
> *While they treat us so cruel!*
> *We must raise our paws,*
> *For fair treatment by laws!*

And so that night, they developed a plan.

The next morning, Sam went to practice with The Gold Mush. Rather than go to the back of the pack, Sam grabbed the front harness.

When Sour-Toe came along, Sam refused to move. He stood with his ears and tail in the air. He barked:

No matter what colour,
No matter what breed,
All huskies deserve,
A fair chance to lead!

News soon spread to the Ministry of Dogsled Affairs.

Officer Pawmela arrived at the practice. She defended her selection of Sour-Toe. She argued that grey huskies were much too slow to lead.

She said:

> *As all huskies know, grey dogs are too slow,*
> *They've never won gold in the Yukon snow!*

That's why Sam wasn't chosen to lead.

Sled Security arrived moments later. They demanded that Sam go to the back of the pack.

But Sam refused to move.

He barked:

> *No matter what colour,*
> *No matter what breed,*
> *All huskies deserve,*
> *A fair chance to lead!*

Sled Security took poor Sam HusGee to the dog pound.

That night, Sam was forced to remain behind bars without a bone to chew on. Through the bars of his dark cell, he watched an episode of *George Strombone Tonight*.

As he watched, he howled out to the starless sky.

That night, Dogavan e-mailed all of the grey huskies in the Yukon.

The subject read:

Stop chasing cars, our friend Sam's behind bars!

And the message said:

Every hound around, please join me at the pound!
We'll bark against injustice and make lots of sound!

The next morning, Sam HusGee awoke to the sound of dozens of dogs barking. He looked through the bars of his cell. A large group of huskies had gathered.

They were all howling in support of his cause.

They howled:

> *No matter what colour,*
> *No matter what breed,*
> *All huskies deserve*
> *A fair chance to lead!*

The grey huskies refused to participate in The Yukon Quest. They wouldn't run until grey huskies were treated fairly by the Ministry.

That day, a copy of *The Globe and Trail* was delivered to the Ministry of Dogsled Affairs.

Officer Pawmela read the cover story:

> *Breaking news, hot off the trails,*
> *Has got some huskies waving their tails.*
> *Grey huskies refuse to run the Quest,*
> *They've not run a race since Sam's arrest!*
> *This morning at the pound*
> *All hounds gathered round,*

And barked:

> *No matter what colour,*
> *No matter what breed,*
> *All huskies deserve*
> *A fair chance to lead!*

Officer Pawmela knocked her cup of coffee on the floor.

There was puppy panic at the Ministry. Officer Pawmela stared at all of the newspapers on the table.

As they debated what to do, Sour-Toe entered the Ministry's front doors.

Even though he wanted to lead The Gold Mush, Sour-Toe knew that he wasn't the fastest on the team. He handed his harness to Officer Pawmela.

Sour-Toe knew that Officer Pawmela hadn't followed the Lead Dog Rule properly. She hadn't chosen the fastest husky on the team.

As Sam looked out of his cell, he was amazed at how many dogs had gathered.

He was even being talked about on *George Strombone Tonight*.

The host, George Strombone, said:

> *The Ministry has gotten itself into a mess!*
> *It's written all over the Canadian Press.*
> *The grey huskies have an important gripe.*
> *The officer applied a stereotype!*

There was an emergency meeting at the Ministry.

As the others questioned her, Officer Pawmela finally barked up.

> *You know, maybe they are quite right?*
> *I was convinced of the stereotype!*
> *I assumed Sam was slow because he's grey,*
> *And didn't consider him on selection day.*

And so the Ministry agreed to correct the whole mess.

Later that day, Sam HusGee was released from the pound.

As he stepped out of his cell, he barked:

> Whether fur is golden, spotted or brown,
> All huskies deserve respect in this town!
> Laws must be managed in a way that is fair,
> With no dog overlooked because of his hair!

The Ministry changed the way it selected lead dogs.

Soon after, the Ministry held competitions to see who was the fastest husky on each team. This way, all huskies would have a fair chance to be lead dog.

During the competition to choose the leader of The Gold Mush, Sam HusGee sped by his teammates. Sour-Toe smiled as he watched Sam mush through the snow!

And that day, the Ministry chose Sam HusGee as the first grey husky to lead a team in The Yukon Quest.

Sam lead The Gold Mush that year with his ears held high. For many miles, he mushed through the snow.

As Sam approached the finish line, all the huskies wagged their tails in the air!

The Gold Mush came in third place.

Even though his team did not finish first, Sam felt like he had won the real Yukon Gold. Grey huskies were finally being treated fairly.

The next day, it wasn't the winner of The Yukon Quest that made the front page. It was Sam HusGee.

The front page of *The Globe and Trail* read:

> *There are strange things done in the daylight sun,*
> *By the huskies who mush for gold.*
> *The Arctic trails have their doggy tales,*
> *Like the one that was just told.*
>
> *The Northern Lights have seen great sights,*
> *But the greatest they ever did see,*
> *Was that day on the trails with waving tails,*
> *No one discriminated against Sam HusGee!*

Note for Parents and Teachers:

This story seeks to teach children about the right to equal treatment and freedom from discrimination on the basis of race, which is guaranteed by section 15(1) of the *Canadian Charter of Rights and Freedoms*. This section provides that:

> *Every individual is equal before and under the law and has the right to the equal protection and equal benefit of the law without discrimination and, in particular, without discrimination based on... colour [or] race.*[1]

Historically, many Canadian laws and government actions discriminatorily targeted specific racial groups. Some notable examples include the laws that sanctioned the Chinese head tax, the restriction of Black and Jewish immigration, and the internment of Japanese Canadians during World War II. In more recent years, Canada has made much progress in fostering a more multicultural and inclusive society. Today's laws, for example, are largely colourblind—they no longer distinguish or mistreat on the basis of race or colour.[2]

In spite of this progress, racial discrimination has and will persist. Laws do not exist apart from a colour-conscious society—even though laws may be colourblind, people are not.[3] For example, those administering the laws can continue to apply stereotypes to discriminate on the basis of race and colour. Canadians must therefore be vigilant in addressing instances of unfair treatment to ensure equality is realized.

In this story, Sam HusGee is the victim of the unfair administration of the law. There was no formal rule or law that excluded grey huskies from leading a dogsled team. Much like today's laws, the Lead Dog Rule was colourblind. Instead of the rule itself being discriminatory, it was the agent administering the law who was discriminatory in her selection of lead dogs. Officer Pawmela overlooked Sam HusGee as the fastest husky in the pack because of the stereotype that grey huskies were slow. She therefore discriminated against him on the basis of his colour.

This story seeks to demonstrate that equality is not an achievement of any particular moment in time. It was not achieved, for example, on the day in which grey huskies were finally allowed to mush on the Yukon Trail.

Likewise, equality was not achieved when Canada embraced multiculturalism and a more inclusive society with the adoption of the *Canadian Charter of Rights and Freedoms*. Instead, equality requires vigilance and persistence. Instances of unfair treatment must be continually confronted and challenged.

Sam's refusal to go to the back of the pack is a demonstration of the vigilance that is required to confront instances of racial mistreatment. The act of civil disobedience, the boycott of the Yukon Quest, and the negative media surrounding the incident, forces the Ministry to respond. They force the administration to treat all colours (and breeds) of dogs in a fair manner. The realization of equality requires such courage and vigilance—it requires the continual pursuit of *real* Yukon gold.

Questions for children:

1. Was it fair that Sam wasn't considered to lead The Gold Mush? Why or why not?

2. What is the stereotype in this story? What are some examples of stereotypes you've heard in your own life? Can you think of a time when you mistreated someone because of a stereotype?

3. Why is Sam taken to the dog pound? Why do other dogs show up to support him?

4. At the end of the story, why does Sam make the front page of the paper even though his team only came in third place in The Yukon Quest?

---

[1] *Canadian Charter of Rights and Freedoms,* s 15(1), Part I of the *Constitution Act,* 1982, being Schedule B to the *Canada Act* 1982 (UK), 1982, c 11.

[2] Bruce Ryder, Cidalia Faria and Emily Lawrence, *"What's Law Good For? An Empirical Overview of Charter Equality Rights Decisions"* (2004) 24 *Supreme Court Review* 103 at 25.

[3] Patricia J. Williams, *"The Obliging Shell (An Informal Essay on Formal Equal Opportunity)"* in *After Identity: A Reader in Law and Culture* (New York: Routlege, 1995) at 121.